BESTEST DAD EVER

summersdale

BESTEST DAD EVER

Summersdale Publishers Ltd
46 West Street
Chichester
West Sussex
PO19 1RP
UK

www.summersdale.com

Printed and bound in China

ISBN: 978-1-84953-133-7

Substantial discounts on bulk quantities of Summersdale books are available to corporations, professional associations and other organisations. For details contact Summersdale Publishers by telephone: +44 (0) 1243 771107, fax: +44 (0) 1243 786300 or email: nicky@summersdale.com.

To: ....

From: ....

Life doesn't come with an instruction book; that's why we have fathers.

H. Jackson Brown Jr

Being a dad is more important than football.

David Beckham

The toughest job
in the world isn't
being a president.
It's being a parent.

Bill Clinton

Dad taught me everything I know. Unfortunately, he didn't teach me everything he knows.

Al Unser Jr

A father is a man who
expects his children
to be as good as he
meant to be.

Carol Coats

If I wanted something from my father, I would put my little feet together pigeon-toe style, tilt my head and smile. I got what I wanted every time.

Shirley MacLaine

THINGS THAT DADS CAN DO WITH ONE HAND BEHIND THEIR BACK

☆ Carry the family's luggage (including three lilos and a deckchair)

☆ Rescue a favourite ball from the neighbour's guttering

☆ Find a parking spot in the busiest of car parks

☆ Carry sleeping children up to bed without waking them

☆ Fix a broken toy (especially reattaching body parts to action figures and dolls)

☆ Make a den in the garden with old junk from the shed

☆ Simultaneously drink beer, eat crisps and keep other people's hands away from the TV remote

☆ Sneak me a chocolate bar without Mum seeing

When I was a kid, I used to imagine animals running under my bed. I told my dad... He cut the legs off the bed.

Lou Brock

Dads are stone skimmers, mud wallowers, water wallopers, ceiling swoopers, shoulder gallopers, upsy-downsy, over-and-through, round-and-about whoosers.

Helen Thomson

Dad... a son's first hero.

Anonymous

Having one child makes
you a parent; having two
you are a referee.

David Frost

Ask your mother.

Frank Lancaster's advice to his children

My daddy, he was somewhere between God and John Wayne.

Hank Williams Jr

The only way for this father to be certain of bathroom privacy is to shave at the gas station.

Bill Cosby

My daughter wanted a
new pair of trainers.
I told her, 'You're eleven.
Make your own!'

Jeremy Hardy

YOU KNOW YOU'RE A DAD WHEN...

☆ ... you can finish your own meal, plus leftovers, and still make room for one or two of your children's sweets!

☆ ... you remain confident in your navigation skills, even when it's obvious you're completely lost

☆ ... you come back with a bumper pack of Twiglets and a *Top Gear* DVD after Mum asks you to do the weekly shop

☆ ... your child coming third in the egg-and-spoon race is as important as your team winning the World Cup

☆ ... you're not embarrassed to sing (the wrong words) to a hip new song on the radio

☆ ... you can't resist the urge to prove that you've 'still got it' at any family event involving a disco

☆ ... you always volunteer to help with homework – even though you have no idea what a 'square root' is

DAD

Fathering is not
something perfect men
do, but something that
perfects the man.

Frank Pittman

I've made a few nice dishes in my time, but this has got to be the best one I've ever made.

Jamie Oliver talking about his first child

Any man can be a father
but it takes someone
special to be a dad.

Anonymous

You don't raise heroes; you raise sons. And if you treat them like sons, they'll turn out to be heroes, even if it's just in your own eyes.

Walter Schirra Sr

Fatherhood is pretending
the present you love most
is soap-on-a-rope.

Bill Cosby

I have found the best way to give advice to your children is to find out what they want and then advise them to do it.

Harry S. Truman

The sooner you treat your son as a man, the sooner he will be one.

John Dryden

My mother taught me my ABCs. From my father I learned the glories of going to the bathroom outside.

Lewis Grizzard

THINGS THAT ALWAYS MAKE A DAD PROUD

☆ Taking the stabilisers off your bike (even if he has to put them straight back on again)

☆ Watching you tie your own shoelaces (even if you end up tying your fingers, too)

☆ Watching you in the school nativity play (even if you do only play Sheep #6)

☆ Learning that you got a good mark for your homework assignment (even if he did most of the work)

☆ Passing your driving test (even if it cost him an arm and a leg)

☆ Attending your graduation (even if he still has no clue what you were studying)

☆ Seeing you move out into your own place (even if you do take half of the household appliances with you)

☆ Getting a mention in the local paper (even if it is for coming next to last in the church talent show)

DAD

Your dad is the man who does all the heavy shovelling for your sandcastle, and then tells you you've done a wonderful job.

Rose O'Kelly

Dad always called me
his 'favourite son'.

Cameron Diaz on being a tomboy

By the time a man realises that maybe his father was right, he usually has a son who thinks he's wrong.

Charles Wadsworth

A father is a banker
provided by nature.

French proverb

Never put anything on paper, my boy, and never trust a man with a small black moustache.

P. G. Wodehouse quoting his father's advice to him

Small boy's definition of Father's Day: It's just like Mother's Day only you don't spend so much.

Anonymous

It is a wise father that knows his own child.

William Shakespeare

My son complains about headaches. I tell him all the time, when you get out of bed, it's feet first!

Henny Youngman

WAYS DAD WILL ALWAYS EMBARRASS YOU

☆ He'll give you a kiss on the cheek when he drops you off at school in front of your mates

☆ He'll try to sound cool with dodgy references to popular culture... Anyone got the new Lady YaYa album?

☆ He'll ask your new love interest uncomfortable questions about your relationship

☆ ... or he'll tell them all about the time you had to sleep with the light on after watching *Jurassic Park*

☆ He'll tell jokes that only he finds funny

☆ He'll continue to refer to you as 'Pumpkin', 'Sunshine' or any other such childhood nickname until you're at least 40

☆ He'll wear something that stopped fitting him 20 years ago - in public, of course

☆ He'll try to friend you on Facebook

Dad; you're someone to look up to no matter how tall I've grown.

Anonymous

A father is a giant from whose shoulders you can see for ever.

Perry Garfinkel

I think my dad is a lot cooler than other dads. He acts like he's still 17.

Miley Cyrus

When you can't do anything else to a boy, you can make him wash his face.

Ed Howe

Up until I became a father, it was all about self-obsession. But then I learned exactly what it's all about: the delight of being a servant.

Eric Clapton

My father only hit
me once – but he
used a Volvo.

Bob Monkhouse

The place of the father
in the modern suburban
family is a very small one,
particularly if he plays golf.

Bertrand Russell

Noble fathers have
noble children.

Euripides

SECRET SKILLS THAT ONLY DADS KNOW

☆ How to assemble anything, even with Japanese instructions (who reads instructions anyway?!)

☆ How to lose convincingly at every single game he plays with you

☆ How to fix your pram... and your bike... and your car

☆ How to follow a film's plotline, despite having slept through the whole thing

☆ How to pull off the socks, sandals and sunburn look on holiday (well...)

☆ How to make you hear the call for dinner even if you're playing at the end of the street

☆ How to break wind and blame it on the dog/cat/gerbil

DAD

The secret of fatherhood
is to know when
to stop tickling.

Anonymous

A father's words are like a thermostat that sets the temperature in the house.

Paul Lewis

Breastfeeding should not be attempted by fathers with hairy chests... they can make the baby sneeze.

Mike Harding

Fatherly love is the ability to expect the best from your children despite the facts.

Jasmine Birtles

My dad used to spend ages tinkering under the bonnet of his Capri... it would invariably have to be towed to the garage.

Robert Greenway

Telling a teenager the facts of life is like giving a fish a bath.

Arnold H. Glasgow

Being a great father is like shaving. No matter how good you shaved today, you have to do it again tomorrow.

Reed Markham

When I was a kid, I said to my father one afternoon, 'Daddy, will you take me to the zoo?' He answered, 'If the zoo wants you, let them come and get you.'

Jerry Lewis

AWARDS FOR THE 'BESTEST DAD EVER':

☆ Bravery in the Face of Spiders and Other Intimidating Creatures

☆ Friendliest 24-hour Taxi Driver

☆ Best Sean Connery (as James Bond) Impression

☆ Champion Pancake Flipper

 Biggest Bear Hugs

⭐ Loudest Sunday League Football Supporter

⭐ Maker of the Tastiest Bacon Butty

⭐ Lord of the (Dad) Dance

⭐ Bounciest Beer Belly

⭐ Best Corny Joke Teller

What do I owe my father? Everything.

Henry Van Dyke

My father taught me
to work; he did not
teach me to love it.

Abraham Lincoln

The voice of parents is the voice of gods, for to their children they are heaven's lieutenants.

William Shakespeare

There are three stages of a man's life: he believes in Santa Claus, he doesn't believe in Santa Claus, he is Santa Claus.

Anonymous

He opened the jar of pickles when no one else could.

Erma Bombeck on her dad

There is a special place in heaven for the father who takes his daughter shopping.

John Sinor

My dad has always
taught me these words:
care and share.

Tiger Woods

Getting a burp out of your little thing is probably the greatest satisfaction I've come across.

Brad Pitt on his first child

THINGS FOUND IN DAD'S SHED

☆ His secret shrine to Jeremy Clarkson

☆ The football strip he wore at 12 when he played in the Junior League finals at school

☆ A Haynes' manual for a car he sold 15 years ago

☆ The first chapter of a book in progress entitled *101 Uses for Used Batteries*

- ⭐ The novelty tie he got from Grandma at Christmas one year

- ⭐ His prized beer-bottle-top collection

- ⭐ A failed attempt at a 'build your own' crystal radio

- ⭐ Twelve gallons of untouched home brew from a couple of years back

A father's solemn duty is to watch football with his children and teach them when to shout at the ref.

Paul Collins

Well, it's hard to know what to get the man who provides everything.

Michael Feldman on receiving a set of hose nozzles on Father's Day

I looked up to my dad. He was always on a ladder.

David Chartrand

Can you abandon a child along a public highway for kicking Daddy's seat for 600 miles?

Erma Bombeck

Mommy would never divorce Daddy. He's just like one of the family.

Bill Keane

Dads grab themselves a
spoon and dig right
in with you.

Anonymous

My father had a profound influence on me - he was a lunatic.

Spike Milligan

I was always embarrassed because my dad wore a suit... while my friends' parents were punks or hippies.

Shirley Manson

YOU NEVER GET REALLY CROSS WITH ME, EVEN WHEN...

☆ ... I leave sticky fingerprints inside your car

☆ ... I flood the bathroom after leaving the tap running

☆ ... my pet snail somehow finds its way into your shoe

☆ ... I use your favourite football shirt to wipe the dog down after a particularly muddy walk

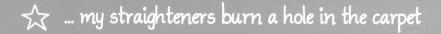 ... my straighteners burn a hole in the carpet

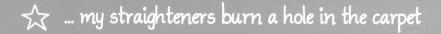 ... I seem incapable of adjusting the volume of my speakers

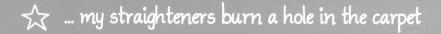 ... I come home with a nose ring and the cast of *Twilight* tattooed on my back

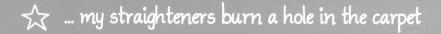 ... I call you up at 3 a.m. to come and pick me up from a party

Infinite patience, boundless enthusiasm, kindness, the ability to score a goal... and the strength to say 'NO' every now and again.

Piers Morgan on what it takes to be a good father

Dads regard themselves
as giant shock absorbers,
there to protect the family
from the ruts and bumps
on the road of life.

W. Bruce Cameron

There's a time for being
a rock star... but you've
got to put time aside for
being daddy, and getting
chocolate rubbed
in your face.

Noel Gallagher

My dad always had this little sign on his desk: 'The bigger your head is, the easier your shoes are to fill.'

Phil Jackson

Never raise your hand to your kids. It leaves your groin unprotected.

Red Buttons

Kids used to come up to me and say, 'My dad can beat up your dad.' I'd say, 'Yeah? When?'

Bill Hicks

My dad was a mean man,
he hypnotised my mother
not to order a starter.

Harry Hill

The father is concerned with parking space, the children with outer space and the mother with closet space.

Evan Esar

It is amazing how quickly the kids learn to drive a car, yet are unable to understand the lawnmower... or vacuum cleaner.

Ben Bergor

I love my dad, although I'm definitely critical of him sometimes, like when his pants are too tight.

Liv Tyler

YOU'RE THE BESTEST DAD BECAUSE...

☆ ... you take me on all the rides at the fair and don't complain when you feel sick

☆ ... you never ask for that fiver I 'borrowed'

☆ ... you let me eat dinner in front of the television

☆ ... you give the warmest hugs

 ... you always BBQ my burger to perfection

 ... you never get tired of telling me the same story at bedtime over and over again

 ... you let me make my own mistakes

 ... you let me do things that Mum doesn't!

Thank you for being...

THE BESTEST
DAD EVER!

www.summersdale.com